Fireflies Against Darkness

Poetry

Kendall Johnson

ARROYO SECO PRESS

Logo by Morgan G Robles
morganrobles.carbonmade.com

Arroyo Seco Press

www.arroyosecopress.org

Cover art: Kendall Johnson

ISBN: 978-1-7326911-5-5

This book is dedicated to
my wife, muse, and patient
listener, Susan Ilsley.

Poems

Note to the Reader

When 2020 rolled to a close I was grateful, scarcely imagining that the new year could get worse. Yet media spectacle bombards us every hour with new more frightening atrocities and threat. We fight over what is right, real, or true. We find ourselves driving a rough road through dark night. In the face of the grinding uncertainty that is today, what can we look toward for the courage to continue?

I. WKNX

This morning the heat dome we have been experiencing this week continues, stretching from the Pacific Northwest all the way across the Great Plains to New York. The average temperature today will be twenty degrees above normal. It is July, only mid-way through summer, and this is the fifth such heat wave so far this year. This is Bonnie Palazzo, WKNX radio.

This life, already and forever is—
teetering on the abyss
precious and tenuous

II. St. Anthony's Story

I seek solitude as spiritual discipline. When I entered this desert I expected the heat and cold, the scarcity and discomfort. Now I find myself terrified of the things I can't see, hear but not understand. What is the howling, the noise in the night? What if I fall and am injured or sick? What if I can't find water?

My loneliness overwhelms. Dreams and delusions haunt both my nights and day. I obsess, I hallucinate. I see things I desire coming toward me, taunting me, then disappearing into air. I ruminate, I remember failures, insults, all the ways I fall short. The hardest I face is the temptation to cover up, to shut down and lose myself.

Out here, the line between imagination and madness grows thin. Yet as I unwrap the city from me, the trappings, distractions, the conditioned wants, the threats and demands, I find myself within.

III. KRLA

Good evening, Los Angeles. Rich Donavich, KRLA news. Today
Los Angeles Public Health officials reported 3,058 new cases of
Coronavirus, a troubling pattern since the June 15 reopening. New
cases over the past seven days are up 80% over the previous seven
day period. While L.A. County is large, there are well over three
thousand county jurisdictions in the U.S., and California has a
relatively low rate of COVID.

Few miles left
smelling Eucalyptus earth;
our evening approaches.

IV. Benjamin's Story

Used and abused as a First Nation child, raised in a violent reformatory. He of lines delicate despite tremors, a beauty compromised by rage. The familiar scene of jail, loud iron doors slamming, the catcalls, the hate, muttered threats, and the beatings. This time Benjamin Chee Chee, a world class talent, hanging dead in his cell at age thirty-three.

A sad truth he lived: wanting permanence, significance now and forever. Yet here's what we are all left with: our lives only long when they are ugly, and too short when good. Fighting for dignity and place in an unjust world, yet somehow Benjamin succeeds for a brief moment: a shooting star against night sky, a swallow in flight.

V. The Nation

Troubling news from the Transportation Security Administration, the agency originally formed in the aftermath of the 2001 attack on the World Trade Center and Pentagon, to keep airline travel safe from terrorists. The TSA this week testified to Congress that by July this year they had already caught 2,807 passengers trying to carry a gun on board a flight in their carry-on bag or on their person. That averages nearly 500 per month. They also report there have been more that 70 physical assaults by passengers on TSA officers.

Gathering darkness,
stories of storm, and fire;
yet promise of midnight stars.

VI. Florence's Story

Crimea, Winter, 1854
We lie in darkness. Medical evacs from the front, we'd been
trucked and sailed to Scutari, near Constantinople, and here we lie.
During the day the few nurses there are can't keep up with the
waves of new arrivals: there's no time to shift us around, surgeons
come to our beds and mattresses on the floor to work. We listen to
each other's pain, the gurgles, cries and shrieks as bones are sawed
and parts removed. The sudden silence, and the muttered, "Let's
move on."

After hours and the rats and ticks come to feed, we try to keep our
moans down, that others might catch an hour's sleep. In midst of
that darkest night, when we all contemplate our endings, she
would come. She brings a lantern, adjusts our bandages, checks on
us.

Much later, I heard newspaper stories of her return home. How
she got off the train on the wrong side, and walked off alone, to
avoid the brass band, speeches and crowd. How she'd gone on to
write books and lecture professors, and even start a nursing school.
She was driven to pass on what she'd learned in Scutari, between
her bouts of bedridden fever. I read how Ms Nightingale was
forever driven by nightmares and terror, yet pushed herself on,
that lady with the lamp.

VII. Boise Night Live

The National Interagency Fire Center announced today that there are currently 88 large wildfires currently burning in the U.S., totaling over a million and a half acres, or nearly 2,500 square miles. This is larger than the state of Delaware.

Disappearing wild;
a piece of land above town
now protected, pristine.

VIII. Ida's Story

Georgia's shouted "You're not good enough!" echoed into Ida's long night. Sister Georgia of the far western spaces, painting labial flowers, and transcendental skulls. Georgia the privileged, who got her leg up in the art world in her marital bed. Georgia who at dinner just tonight told her, "Your life is a waste," and "stay out of my scene!"

"If I only had a Steiglitz," Ida O'Keeffe thought sourly. But she had refused to respond to her brother-in-laws advances, and the easy bridge to the New York galleries had been burned. Now she was leaving the family behind to teach school in California. Another woman erased from art history, almost.

But that night she began the most wonderful dreams. A light house she loved in Cape Cod. It shifted in shape, the colors bold. The energy coming out of it lit more than the night. She dreamed of planets, hanging in new ways in space. Energy fields exploding, rich botanicals turning liquid. Architectural angles, with lines of force. Dynamic symmetry, but impossibly true.

Ida's midnight salvation demanded to be poured onto canvas.

IX. Albuquerque Tribune.

The pandemic is playing havoc in the state of Missouri, which now has the second highest number of COVID cases in the country. The death count due to COVID-19 in Missouri has now topped 100,000.

Quieting descends.
Imagine sheltering
there off in the trees.

X. Chuck's Story

Rounding the corner in the big art museum, I come face to face
with a crowd. They stand and stare past me at the tall wall behind.
I look around and glance up into a sea of small squares all over a
huge canvas. Each square a miniature abstract. Yet seen from
across the room, an enormous person stares back.

Chuck Close, the master of blemish, bruise, and infinite gaze. A
poster boy of neural disorder, he grew up weak and dyslexic. He
had a strange unrelated disorder that left him unable to decode
faces. Yet Close persevered to the top of the art scene through
careful planning, technics and a drive to make meaning.

Then, at 40, a great fall. At what might have been his apex, a spinal
stroke. Left quadriplegic, he could have hung up his brushes.
Instead, he developed mechanical aids to help him re-master his
large portraits. A machine raises his huge canvases bit by bit, he
paints by tiny square.

Standing in the darkened hall, the face raises questions in me: How
do you re-knit the world when it slides out from beneath you?

And an answer:
Inch by inch.

XI. St. Louis Dispatch

Tonight it seems a group of Republican state and local officials in the St. Louis, Missouri area are banding together to push back against Missouri health orders. Renewed mask mandates were issued in response to resurgence of COVID-19 and pleas from local health officials and hospitals. The Attorney General stated that such mandates were a restriction on his personal freedom.

Still meadow with trees;
movement betrays camouflage,
the lioness appears.

XII. Kathrine's Story

An artist and history lecturer Katherine's plans were derailed by a
stroke that paralyzed her entire right side. Remembering that it
was art-making that made her most happy, she returned to
painting, even though it was her dominant hand that had been
disrupted by the bleed. More fun now, she finds, when all of it is
experimental. Now she follows where the experiments lead,
explores what she finds, and—incidentally—finds her work quite
sought after.

XIII San Francisco Chronicle

The Calder Fire has entered South Lake Tahoe basin, and evacuation orders for the area have been issued. This is the second fire in recorded history to have completely crossed the Sierra Nevada range from west to east. The Dixie Fire was the first; it started last month. California Office of Emergency Service reported at 7:00 am Tuesday, August 15, that the Calder Fire is being fought by 415 fire engines, 74 water tenders, 25 helicopters, 82 hand crews, 92 bulldozers, "numerous air tankers from throughout the state," for a total of 3,904 personnel from some 50 separate agencies. Residents have been reluctant to evacuate, not believing the flames could reach them.

Eucalyptus towers
resplendent evening glow;
birds heading toward nests.

XIV. Alisha's Story

When I took that art class, I didn't expect much. I found some of my friends there—most Crips from my project. The teacher gave us art materials to work with, but let us do what we wanted. Every morning, we showed up, some of the girls brought their babies. Teacher showed us book about Gee's Bend, and their quilting circles. We shared stories among ourselves, some about the neighborhood, our lives, sometimes the past or our futures. We'd try new stuff the teacher showed us. Mainly, though, we learned from each other, and helped each other try new things. And we'd keep showing up; couldn't let each other down. Explain if we were gone. We even hung an exhibit of our work at the end of the term. They told us more people showed up for our show, than they had all year.

XV. CBS News Tonight

So far five fire engines and one team leader have been sidelined and quarantined for positive COVID tests on the Calder Fire, where the situation is dire and every firefighter important. Fire officials have directed all news personnel to wear masks to the briefings, whether they "feel comfortable or not."

Broken bowl repaired
now stronger at the broken places;
symmetry redefined.

XVI. Wolff's Story

Not only did my parents want the best for me, and from me.
Admonitions rained down: "Strive," "Win," "Achieve." All
purchased at high cost. It wasn't until I failed, and went on to live,
that I could see stars in the night sky. I marvel at *Kitsugi*, the
Japanese art form built upon circumstance. Dropped pottery,
chipped, cracked, or broken in its encounters with the world, can
be repaired with lacquer laced with gold. The resulting piece
becomes stronger, more beautiful than the original. Events leading
to the break become less important, less lamentable, than the
promise revealed. Cracked and jagged edges become golden
histories and new songs, tales of the journey of the piece,
counterpoint to limitations assumed. They speak the
transformation possible for us all.

XVII. Reuters

Ida hit as a category 5, with winds to 150 miles per hour. Global climate change leads to deep warm water rising. The interaction results in the intensification of the storm. The extra16-foot sea level smashed inland, the highest flooding in 150 years. The media is now full of images of flash flood and tornado damage due to Hurricane Ida's path northward and inland to New Jersey and New York, where buildings collapsed, basement and ground level apartments and subways flooded.

Guitar skin forms veneer
over sufficient cavity;
mouth's hidden resonance.

XVIII. Doug's Story

We gathered in his cabin, the twelve of us. Doug was a musician, storyteller, a poet—a truth-teller. We were there to learn to chant. After some warm-ups, he explained how we were going to do something we'd never done before. A form of chanting practiced by Tibetan Buddhists, a form we'd only seen in documentaries.

Doug got us all holding a low tone, then, by allowing air to resonate on our nasal passages, we could cultivate an overtone at the same time. Within a few minutes, most of us were able to hold two pitches at once. There we were, in a cabin among the redwoods, with just our voices, evoking a simultaneous double reality.

XIX. Washington Post

A high school, a middle school, and an elementary school in Tennessee, were forced into lockdown today, due to gunshots and screaming in the adjacent neighborhood streets. Lockdown was lifted when police reported that it was only a gender-reveal party. The newborn would be a boy.

Evening color richens,
quiet moment's eloquence;
sweet light nearly lost.

XX. Clemency's Story

It wasn't the mathematical purity that drew Clemency Burton-Hill back to Bach, as she fought back from her debilitating stroke. Relearning to speak, to sit up and swallow and reach for things, while barely clinging to life itself, she listened to Bach. Clemency rediscovered what Pablo Casals and Albert Schweitzer had said, and what she herself had written the year before, about Bach's healing magic. At first she couldn't listen because Bach's emotionality and depth were too much. Then she gradually began to reclaim the Bach within her. She finally began to play. Every day she would begin to feel her molecules start to sing.

XXI. Christian Science Monitor

A thousand gun deaths in the US last week. Over forty three thousand last year. Americans bought over 23 million guns in 2020; a figure reported by the gun industry itself. If this were Ireland, we'd call it a new level of "troubles." If the Middle East, we'd call it rampant terrorism. If this were a country south of our border, we'd shrug and call it expected. But when it occurs just down the street or the next town over, our eyes close.

Evening comes in shadow;
bold animals of the day retreat,
coyotes sound a nocturne.

XXII. John's Story

The artist leans into his work. He's lost himself in a world unfolding on a foot square piece of paper. Ink lines define a new world emerging from the sea. A sun rising from the city matches that in the sky. Clouds propped by light beams, air currents concrete, marked by histories implied.

He imagines the colors he will add later at home, from warm reds and yellows jumping off the page, to the blues and greens that recede. The purples of forces usually unseen.

A sudden breaking of a water glass shakes him back, to the now world of pandemics, breakdowns, *realpolitiks*. The grinding fear of uncertainty. Glancing up at the clock, he realizes he's been lost, this time, in a coffee shop.

XXIII. Time Magazine

In response to the summer resurgence of COVID hospitalizations and deaths, the U.S. Center for Disease Control reversed their recommendations to relax mask mandates, suggesting that local jurisdictions consider mask mandates again until the Delta Variant is controlled.

While an infection spreads, the Governors of fifteen states have unilaterally banned the local governments in their states from reintroducing mask mandates, overriding city or county authority to make health decisions for their citizens. Infection spreads.

Moon rises
dog calls in the dark;
essence of juniper.

XXIV. Vincent's Story

After the tangle he'd made of his life, van Gogh retreated. From his self-quarantine in the asylum in St. Remy, he would rise on sleepless moonlit nights and peer out his window toward the mountains to the south. He'd look at the cypress trees stretching upward, how they reached toward the moon and sky beyond. The night was alive and full of stars. Vincent reached for his pipe and brushes.

XXV. Huffington Post

I interviewed a COVID ICU nurse, who talks about what her dying patients said when asked why they chose not to vaccinate or mask, just who they believed when they balked. How she holds up I-Pads for them to say their good-byes to families, when they take leave, for their very last time.

Falling stars
invisible guests;
dust landing.

XXVI. Grace's Story

Grace was always making plans. Abused by a stepfather, then a husband, then a landlord, then a boss, she'd finally gone to ground. She'd worked in the art world as an educator, director, and curator, but someone would become her oppressor and she'd pack up and move on. Now, with her funds dangerously low, she considered a life on the street. Then a friend told her about ReCover Village. She scraped together enough to purchase a used tiny house, and had it moved onto her newly leased lot in the desert southwest. The small town didn't look like much on the map, but the circle of women who lived there were a community. Working late in the evening fixing up the place, she'd step out to see the stars. Smelling the sage and creosote, Grace thought about the coming sunrise.

XXVII. The Guardian

The National Hurricane Center warned the east coast of "Significant and widespread flooding," from the incoming storm, Ida. Some listened, some did not. Dozens died, most in downstairs apartments. Politicians are beginning to echo the weather scientists in calling for significant changes in preparedness for extreme weather. So far none of them have given up their limousines or mansions. Nor have they nationalized health care so that the poor don't do most of the dying.

Dark sanctuary
small candles;
many sit waiting.

XXVIII. Wendy's Story

She'd been asked to play a friends's memorial service, and of
course she had agreed. An organist, her music had been her life,
and the family had requested her signature piece. Widor's Toccata
in D7 minor was difficult at best, but rumbled up to a triumphal
intensity. That was a month ago, when Wendy's cancer hadn't yet
gone into her brain. But now that her own fight was drawing to a
close; the chemo eclipsed her thinking, her motor planning was
failing. She couldn't walk, or use the foot pedals necessary for the
piece, though she had figured a way to compensate. It had hurt to
ask her husband to carry her into the church on the night of the
service, to prop her up and hold her in place so she wouldn't fall.
Whatever small errors in the service music occurred were simply
not noticed by those who listened closely.

XXIX. Idaho State Journal

A ten year old boy sits in the car waiting. He caught his sister's cold. Coughing, feverish, he is bald from chemotherapy. His blood counts are going wild. He tries to hold on to a fitful sleep, and his parents are panicked. The hospital is full, he may not be seen — there's no place else to go. Beds are filled with COVID patients struggling to live. Cars drive by full of individuals exercising their rights.

Road through the night
destination unclear;
how best do we drive?

XXX. Laura's Story

Laura drives her small hybrid out into the wild. She parks in a quiet roadside rest. She puts up a sunshade and arranges a camp table and chair. Laura plugs her laptop into her portable solar collector, and sits with her coffee. Then she listens. Often her muse comes through voices of birds, sometimes in rain or waves crashing. Other times it's children's voices, or the singing of truck tires passing on down the highway. Songs become her poems and stories of the world.

She hears the tales of the sensate beings she finds living around her as she writes. They tell of their joy, how they nestle in a vast matrix, of rocks, fallen branches, the clouds and the wind. All recombinant stardust, who may be sentient in ways Laura doesn't yet understand.

Acknowledgements

I wish to acknowledge assistance of writer John Brantingham, the Inaugural Poet Laureate of Sequoia Kings Canyon National Park, and his group Taking Our Publishing Seriously, and of writer Kate Flannery who provided much encouragement and feedback.

Several of these poems appeared in earlier form in issues of Cholla Needles Press.

Biography

Kendall Johnson, recently retired from his work in teaching, psychotherapy, and consulting on scene with emergency and disaster agencies, now he paints and writes in Southern California. He is the author of *Dear Vincent: An Artist and Psychologist Writes Back to Van Gogh*; the nonfiction *Chaos & Ash*, and *Black Box Poetics: Short Memoirs of Chaos*.

Kendall Johnson's *Fireflies against Darkness* is in the end a bright spot in a world that could seem endlessly painful. The author has seen more evil than any one person should have to see from his tour of Vietnam where young men were asked to savage a country and murder strangers, to New York City during the days of 9/11. Between and after that time, he has made a career of confronting evil through his practice as a trauma psychotherapist. What is extraordinary about him is that rather than being dragged down into that evil, he has fought to see the spots of light in an otherwise chaotic universe and to make them his practice. He has maintained his essential self, and this book is a guide for us to do the same.

—John Brantingham, *Inaugural Poet Laureate, Sequoia Kings Canyon National Park*

In life and in print, Kendall Johnson IS this title and believes in its tiny promises. His words are both heart-breaking and heart-mending—but most of all they encourage hope. No matter how dark the circumstance, man-caused or natural, his beautifully-wrought words are spare beacons, truly *Fireflies Against Darkness*.

—Tracey Meloni, *Writer, Nursing Education*

In this collection, Kendall Johnson displays his keen sense of observation in our human condition during our current chaotic times of darkness. Even when writing about how things couldn't possibly seem worse, the power of his words and the beauty of his haiku portray how the actions of others produce fireflies of hope in all of us.

—Annie Bien, Author of *Plateau Migrations* and *Under Shadows of Stars*

Kendall Johnson is no stranger to pain and chaos. As a former firefighter, Vietnam veteran, and psychologist specializing in crisis management and the treatment of traumatic stress, he has mastered the art of wrestling with tangled lives. He's perfected that art in this latest volume. He unflinchingly shows us the darkness while at the same time revealing exquisite, small tales of individual perseverance, generosity, and strength. The contrast is stunningly inspiring.

—Kate Flannery, Writer of *Ekphrasis for the Sasse Museum of Art*, *poetry*, and *memoir*

When times are tough, like they have been lately, we sometimes need help to get through. Kendall Johnson gives us that in Fireflies Against Darkness. Short hard news pieces are followed by tiny verses that, like fireflies, light the path connecting us to quietly courageous people who, using art or music or nature, bring us hope. Bring us out of the darkness. I love this book!

—Louella Lester, author of *Glass Bricks*

This remarkable, highly original chapbook juxtaposes bulletins from the COVID-pandemic, out of control wildfires, natural disasters, mass shootings, and climate change chaos with glimpses of the famous (and not so famous) denizens of the art world and their struggles, including Chuck Close, Georgia and Ida O'Keeffe, and Vincent Van Gogh. I could not stop reading this mesmerizing collection. I didn't want it to end. Kendall Johnson has written something important, holding up a mirror to our tarnished reality.

—Alexis Rhone Fancher, author of *EROTIC: New & Selected, poetry*, editor, Cultural Daily